COLOR TEST

REPEAT

REPEAT

REPEAT

REPEAT

THIS BOOK
BELONGS TO

REPEAT

REPEAT
REPEAT
REPEAT

Welcome
to
Junkyard

REPEAT

REPEAT

REPEAT

REPEAT

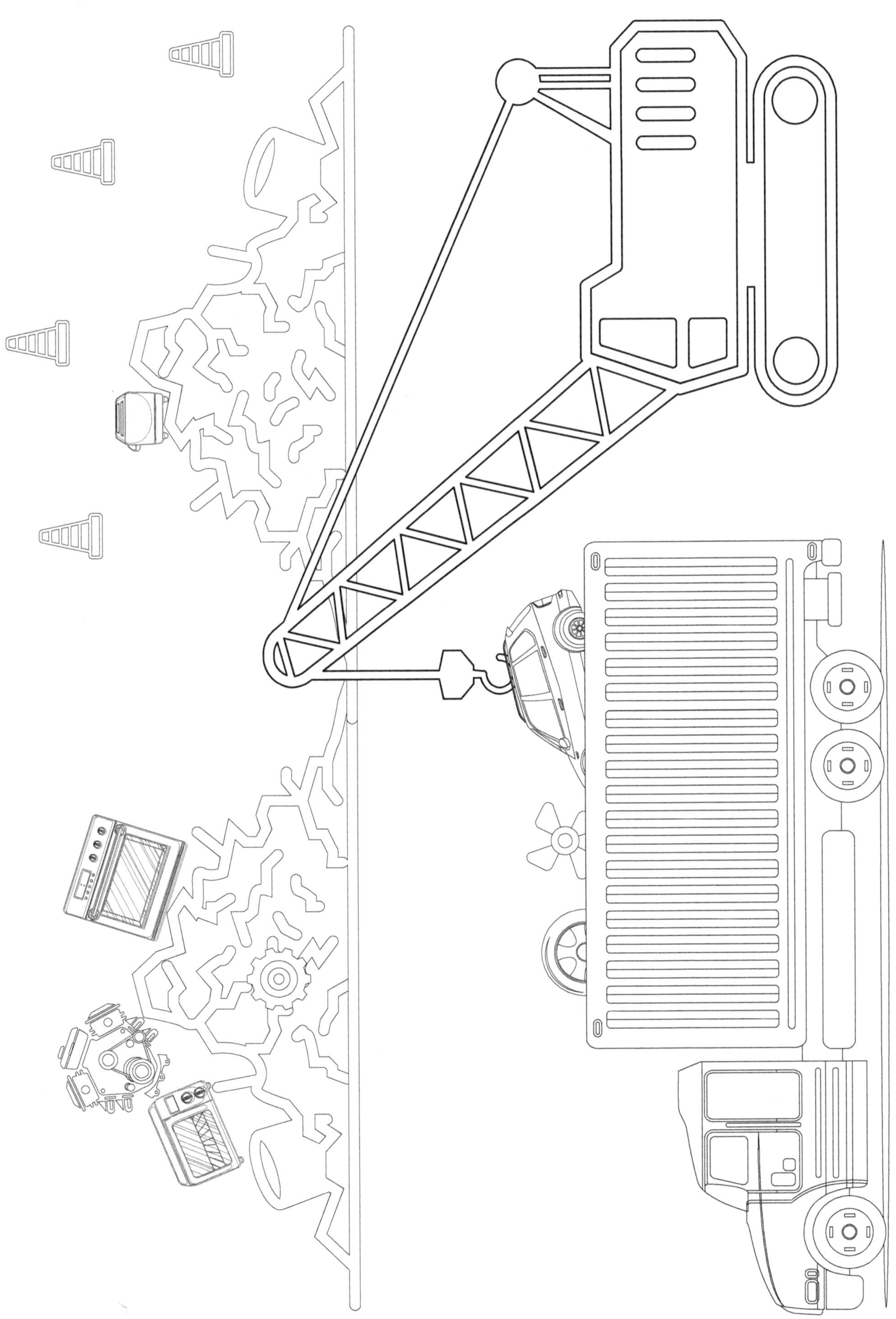

REPEAT

REPEAT

REPEAT

REPEAT

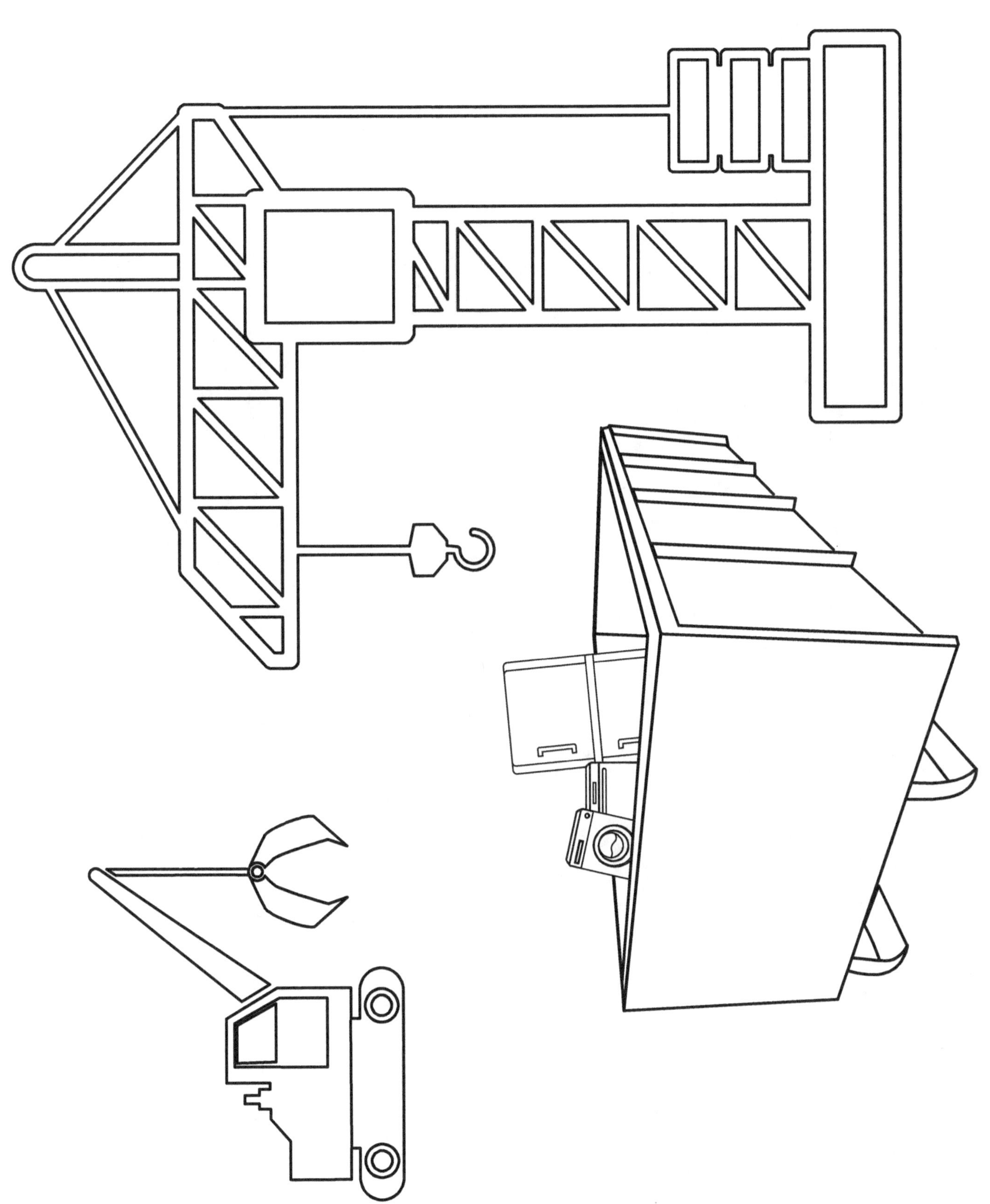

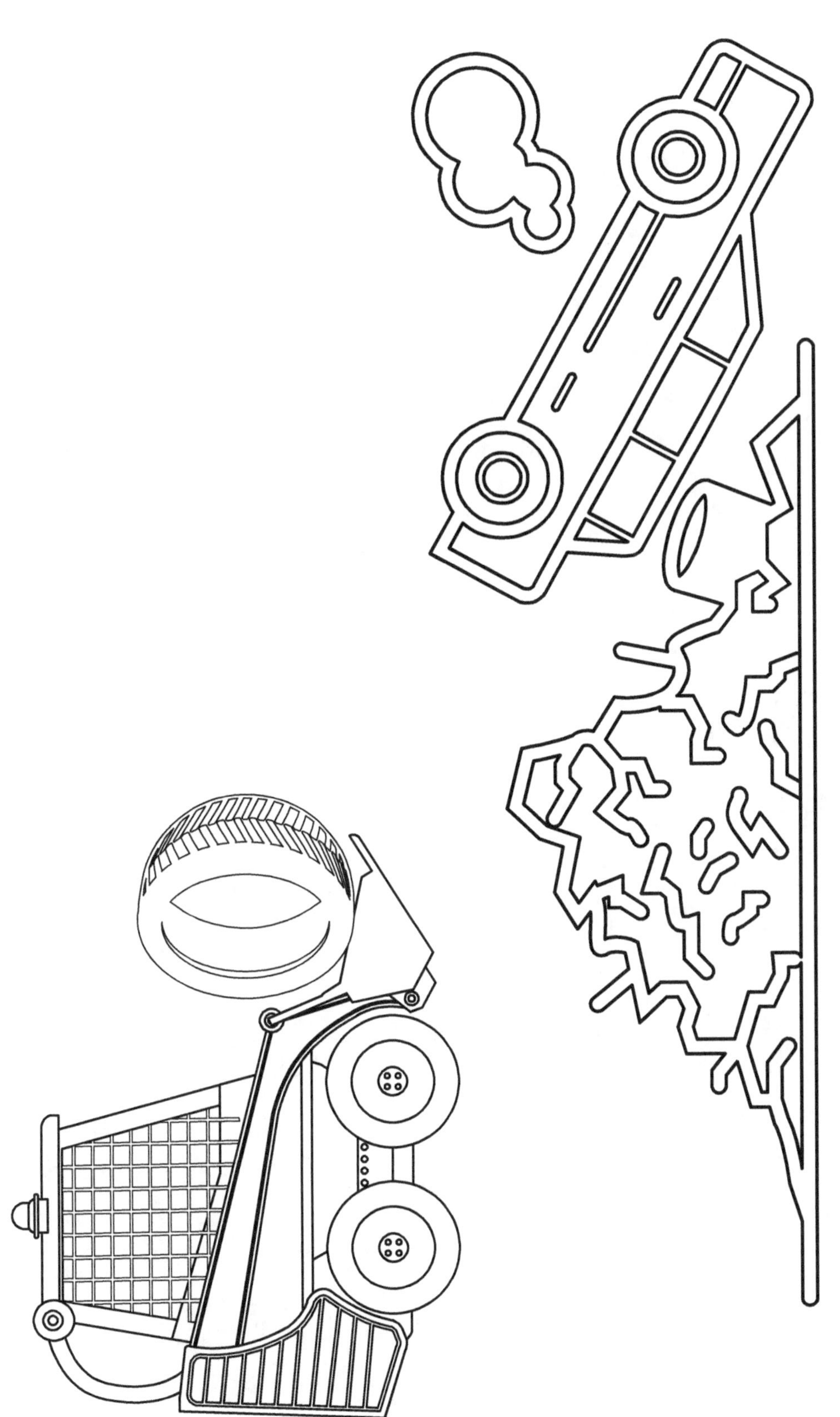

JUNKYARD
Scrap Collector

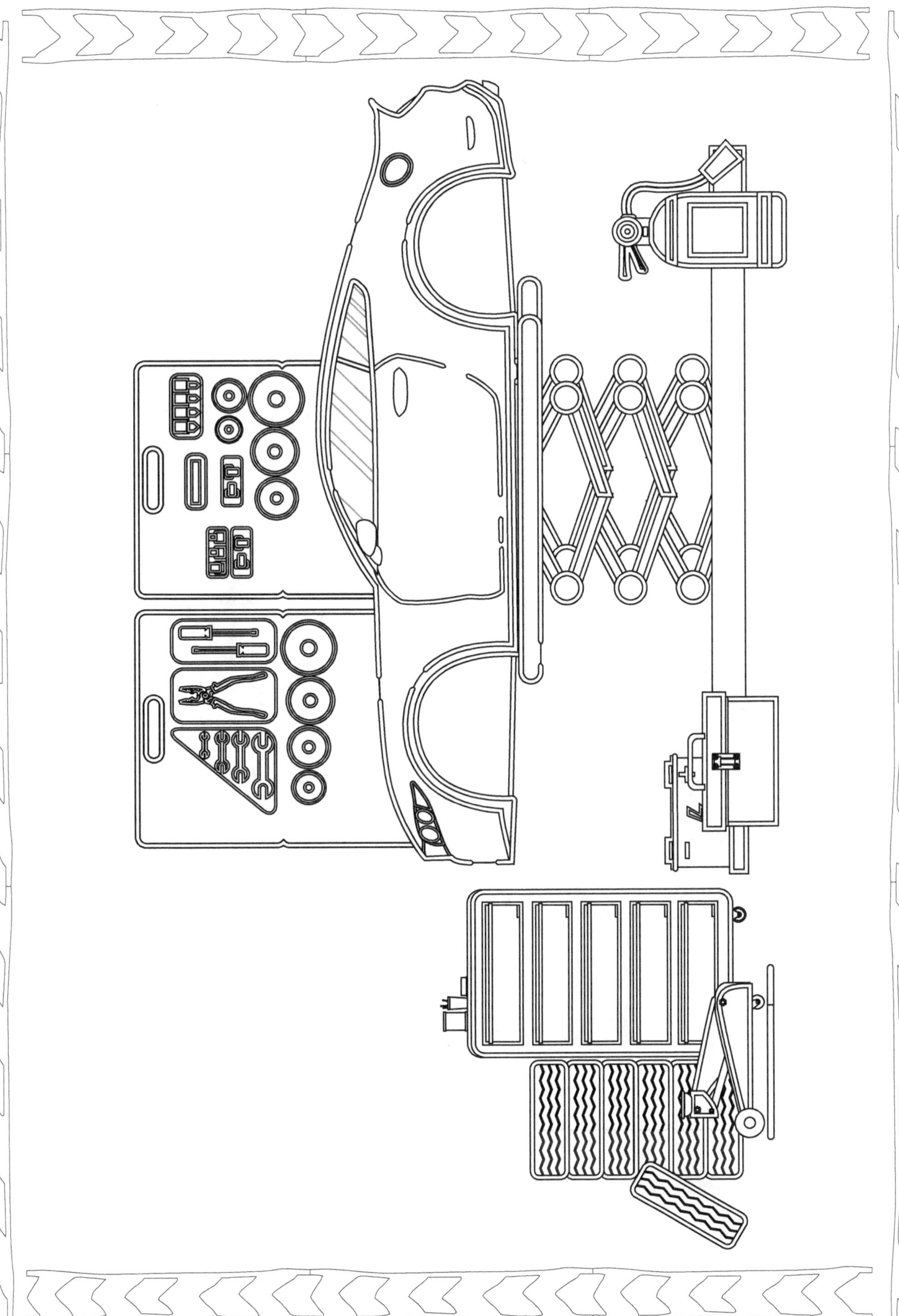

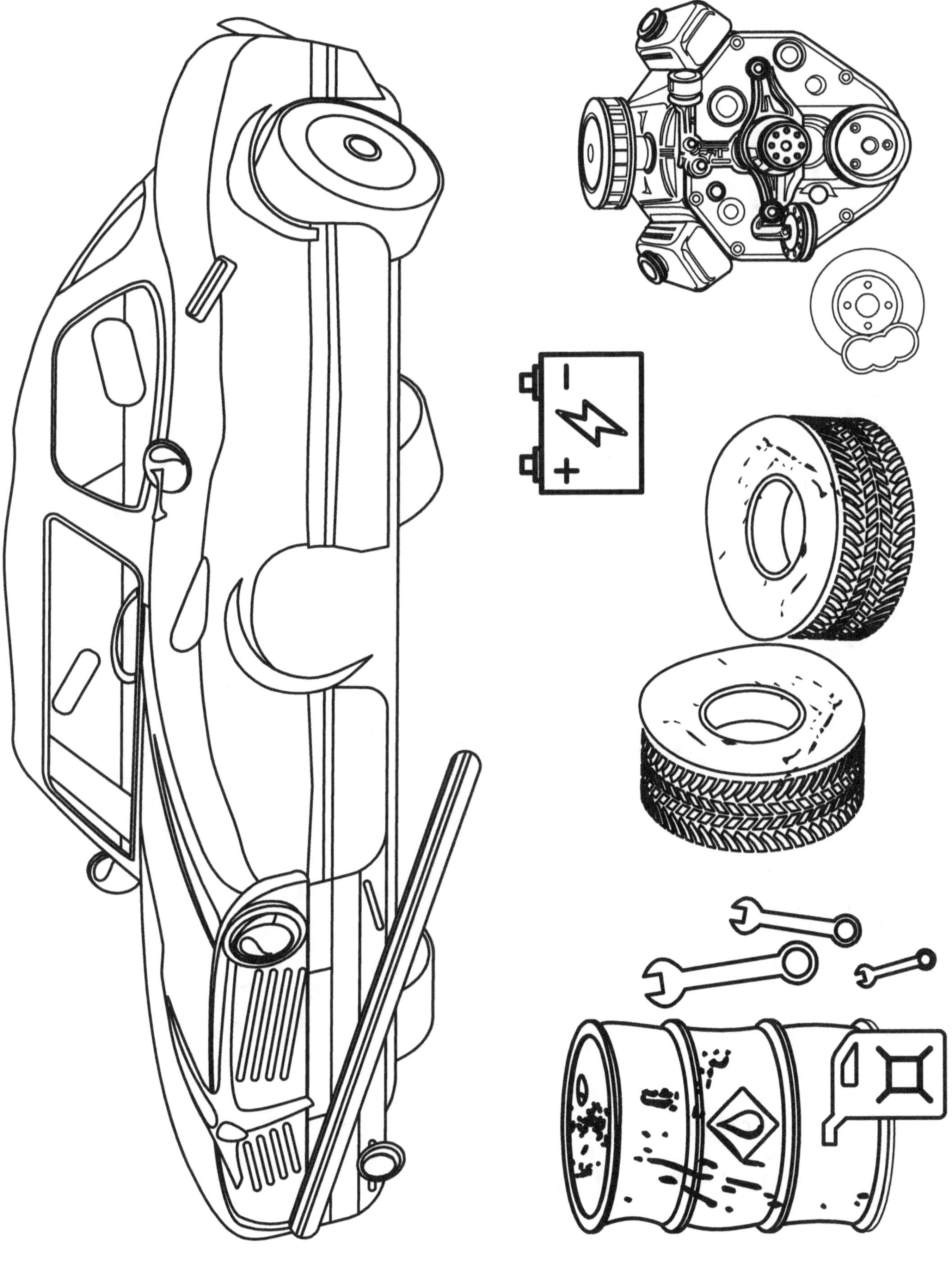

REPEAT

REPEAT

REPEAT

REPEAT

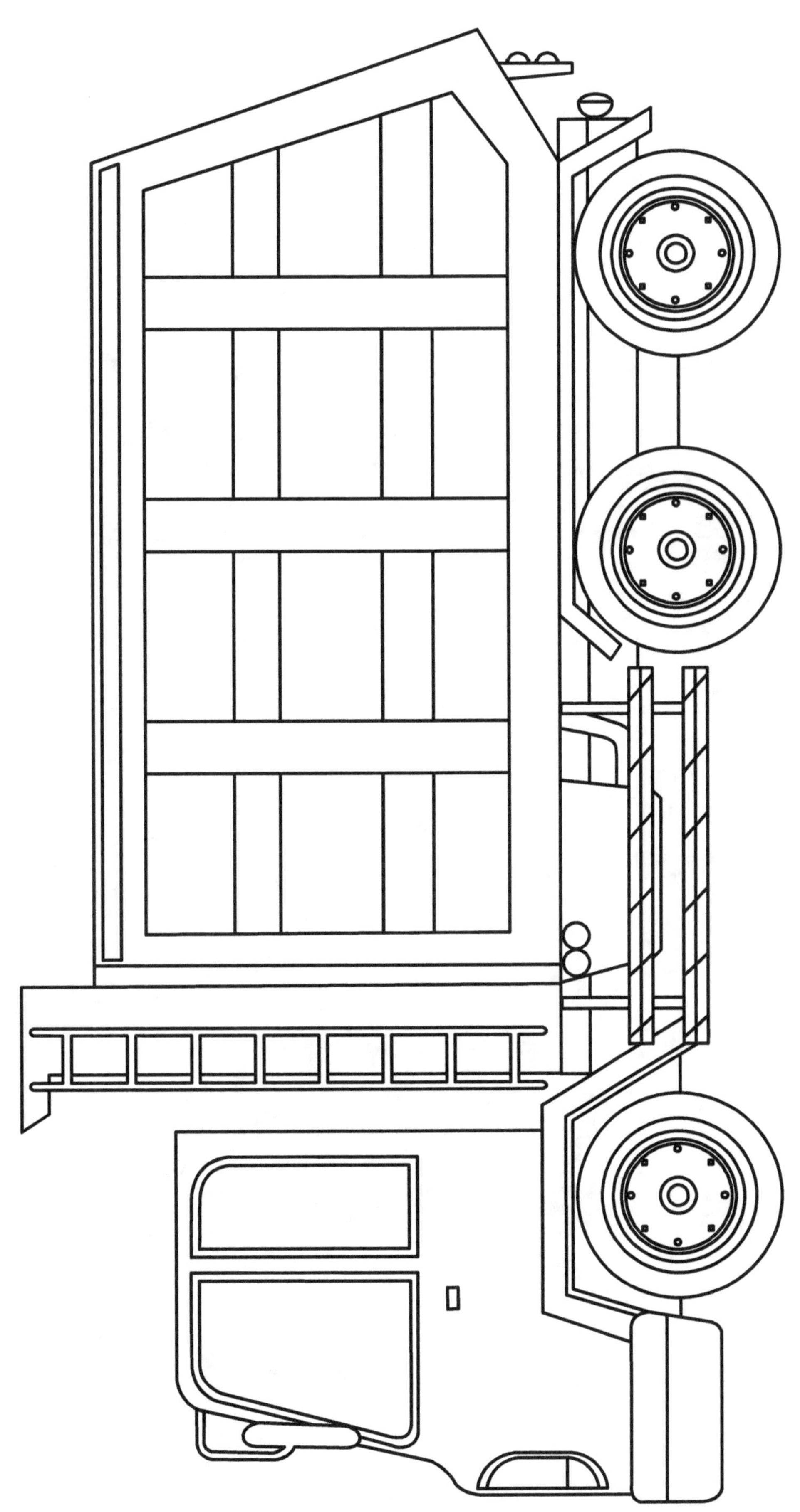

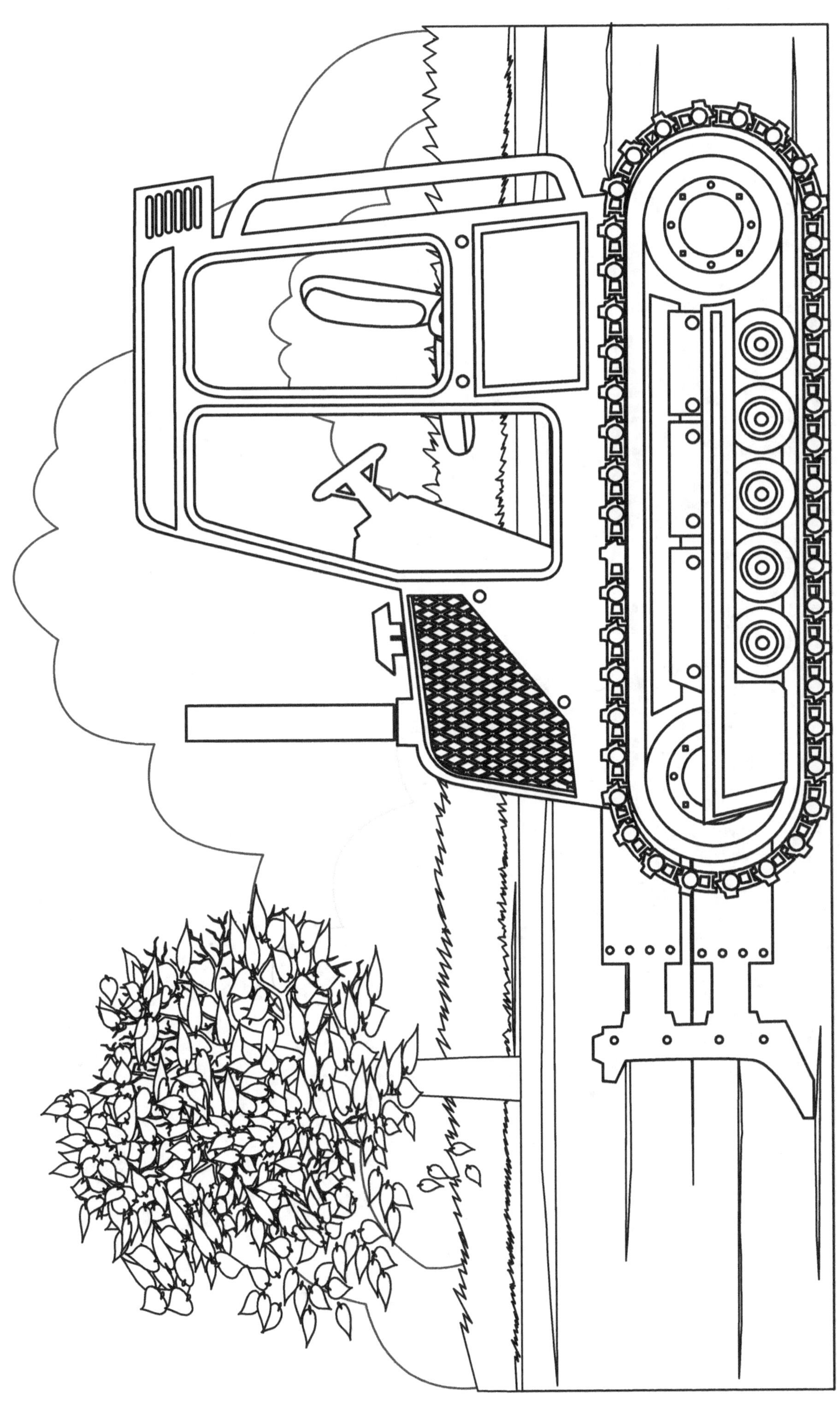

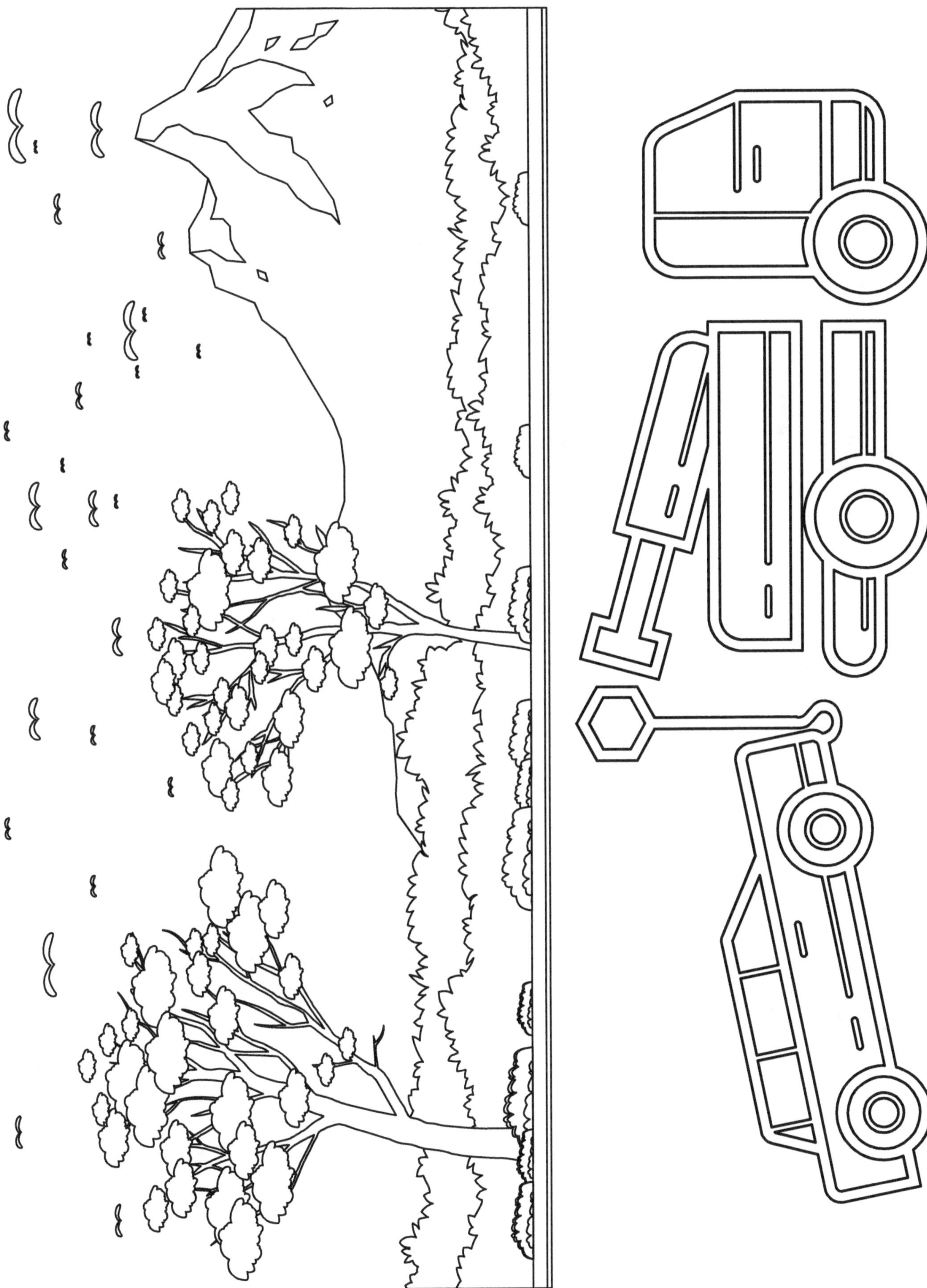

REPEAT

REPEAT

REPEAT

REPEAT

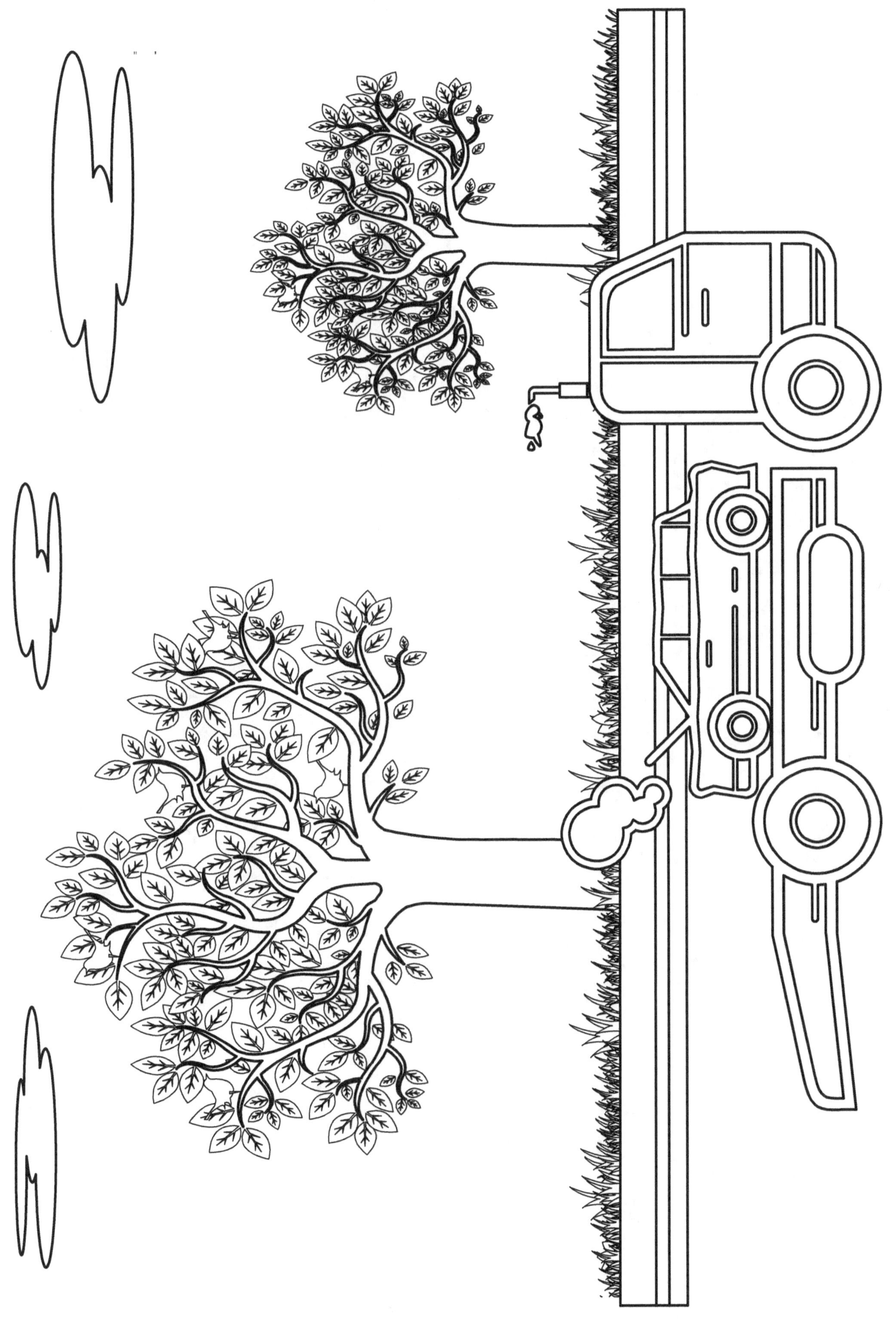

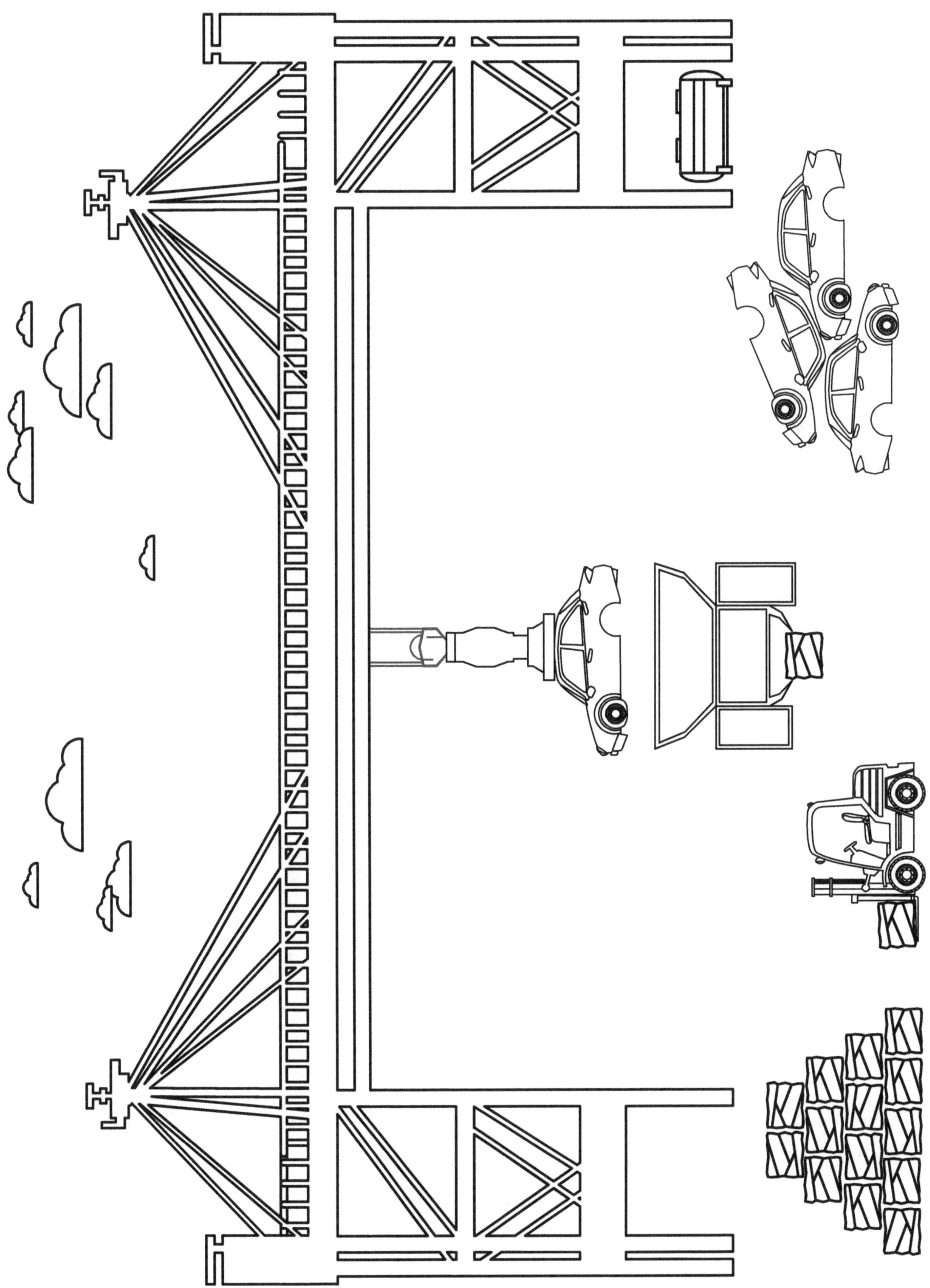

REPEAT

REPEAT

REPEAT

REPEAT

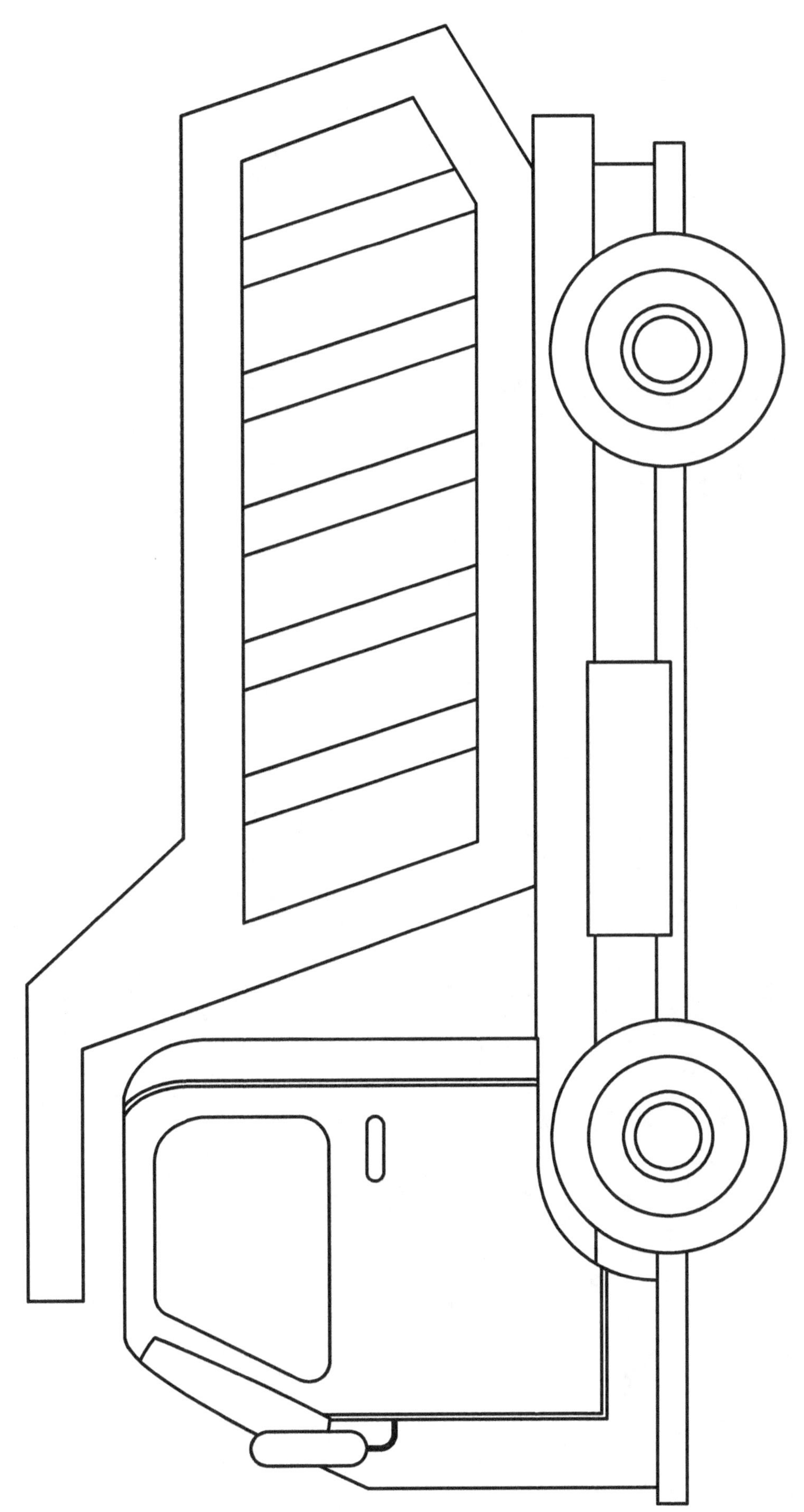

REPEAT

REPEAT

REPEAT

REPEAT